Arch $3.—
FBC
3/20

"*Paint matters! I have long believed that people undervalue the role of paint color in creating community identity, pride, and interest. Gilderbloom's book highlights an overlooked example, the fourth largest collection of painted ladies in the U.S. Louisville is full of surprises, and this one teaches real lessons.*"

— Jeff Speck, City Planner and author of *Walkable City: How Downtown Can Save America, One Step at a Time* and co-author of *Suburban Nation*

"*John Gilderbloom argues that brightly colored buildings are neither new nor a fad of urban gentrifiers. With his finger on examples from several continents, the author shows that sprightly exteriors are signs of vitality, individuality, and a determined pride-of-place. He calls for folks to move beyond their pallet of muted 'historic' colors and to embrace unadulterated brightness. In addition to being an urban mood changer, color, Gilderbloom argues, actually adds value to communities in various states of recovery.*"

— Dr. Tom Owen, University of Louisville Archives, filmmaker on historic preservation practices, and former City Councilmember of the University of Louisville

"Painting houses is a worldwide practice for self-expression. It also cues in that someone of responsibility and concern is around. Color, and its maintenance, can thus be an urban force for confidence. Chromatic Homes takes such concerns seriously and helps us see what, when taken to exuberant forms, can be the delightful result."

— Harvey Molotch, Professor of Sociology, New York University
and author of *The City as a Growth Machine*

"Great neighborhoods are the secret sauce of great cities and communities of all kinds, sizes, and stripes, but great neighborhoods don't happen by accident. They are continuously rebuilt, revitalized, and actively redesigned. They can, and should, be inclusive places where regeneration benefits everyone. Gilderbloom argues that the principles of chromatic design can help us create better neighborhoods and communities. This book is an important contribution to the future of cities."

— Richard Florida, author of *The Rise of the Creative Class* and *The New Urban Crisis*

"Don't let the title fool you. John 'Hans' Gilderbloom's Chromatic Homes: The Joy of Color in Historic Places isn't about paint, or even paint colors. It is about rebuilding communities in which people want to live. And Gilderbloom understands this, having spent his career helping communities rebuild themselves, especially in his beloved Louisville. With examples from around the country and around the world, Hans makes the link between renewing the vibrancy of the historic built environment and renewing the vibrancy of the neighborhood itself. Preservationists will get this immediately. But for those who don't consider themselves 'historic preservationists' this should be required reading. Fine, don't care about heritage buildings, but if you care about urban communities, you should pay attention to what Dr. Gilderbloom is telling you."

— Donovan Rypkema, Principal of PlaceEconomics

"A stroll through the streets of any city should reveal authenticity and evoke joy. And there are few easier ways to distinguish a community's character and personality than finding a 'painted lady' Victorian. We're proud that Louisville is home to so many, and we appreciate the opportunity to showcase how to increase a home's character through the simplicity and power of paint."

— Louisville Mayor Greg Fischer

"John Gilderbloom is an academic rarity. His talents and creativity are expressed not only in the classroom and in peer-reviewed articles, but also in corporate boardrooms and metro councils debating housing, commerce, and land usage. In short, he practices what he preaches. Chromatic Homes is a stellar example of his creative pragmatism and is destined to be read not only by future urban planners and entrepreneurs, but also those intrigued by the concept of architecture as an artist's palette. Read this book and you will experience the 'joy' of these palettes."

— Lyle Sussman PhD, Professor of Management, University of Louisville, a Best-Selling Author, Consultant, Speaker, and Executive Coach

CHROMATIC HOMES

The Joy of Color in Historic Places

John I. "Hans" Gilderbloom

Designed by Leah Callahan and John I. "Hans" Gilderbloom

ISBN: 0-8131-7614-X

Four Colour Print Group - Louisville, Kentucky, USA

Printed in South Korea

Distributed by University Press of Kentucky

663 South Limestone Street, Lexington, KY 40508-4008

kentuckypress.com

1 2 3 4 5 6 7 8 9

First Edition

To contact the author regarding motivational talks on neighborhood revitalization or to purchase a CD for $20 that contains the photos included in this volume along with 200 additional photos, please write to:

Chromatic Homes
c/o Dr. Gilderbloom
Sustainable Urban Neighborhoods, University of Louisville
426 West Bloom Street, Louisville, KY 40208

This book was largely funded by a donation from Larry Gough and Chase Sorrick of Investment Property Advisors, David Day Real Estate, Marilyn Melkonian of Telesis, Jeff Underhill of Underhill Associates, and Louisville City Councilmember David James.

Orders and Customer Service:

Hopkins Fullfillment Service

P.O. Box 50370

Baltimore, MD 21211-4370

Phone: 800-537-5487

hfscustserv@press.jhu.edu

To Donna, my muse.

Chromatic Homes - *How to Ignite a Neighborhood!*

Foreword by Jerry Abramson

Is it possible that an ordinary—vernacular—building can become a neighborhood icon by painting it with bold and lively colors? Can a chromatic home ignite the rest of a neighborhood and sustain it for another generation instead of losing it to abandonment, arson, or the wrecking ball? Can a chromatic home bring joy, pride, hope, renewal, reinvestment, and prosperity?

More people are deciding to choose a place before they choose a job; they are also choosing a passion before they grab a paycheck. Attractive environments and communities are keys to citizen happiness. Thus, we have a social responsibility to pay attention to what makes neighborhoods thrive or die.

Dr. Gilderbloom, who is known as an influential urban thinker, offers lessons to guide neighborhood activists, elected officials, and developers on how to renew declining neighborhoods. The joy of color inspires neighborhoods to flourish and move forward.

Beauty matters. Dr. Gilderbloom shows that making our buildings and streets good-looking goes hand in hand with other factors that revive neighborhoods—preservation, bike lanes, community gardens, walkability, trees, clean air, and traffic calming measures. He contends that chromatic neighborhoods increase home ownership, sustainability, likeability, safety, health, and prosperity.

This book focuses not only on Louisville's success in igniting neighborhoods with paint, preservation, and prosperity, but also on the global influence of color. As the former five-term Mayor of Louisville, I was proud to learn that my city is grouped with San Francisco, CA; Miami, FL; and New Orleans, LA as a viable and cool chromatic place! But also noted are some other unknown and worthy contenders such as Cincinnati, OH; Havana, Cuba; Samara, Russia; Capitola, CA; New Albany, IN; Amsterdam, Netherlands; Covington, KY; Savannah, GA; and Burano, Italy.

Chromatic homes are a social movement happening around the world. They are reclaiming abandoned neighborhoods and serving as a catalyst for urban rejuvenation.

- - - - - - - -

Jerry Abramson was Deputy Assistant to President Obama and Director of Intergovernmental Affairs at the White House.
He served five terms as Mayor of Louisville, and was Lt. Governor of Kentucky.
Jerry is currently Executive in Residence at Bellarmine University.

Imagine San Francisco without "painted ladies."
It would not be San Francisco.

Think of Miami Beach without the colorful Art Deco buildings.

And think about New Orleans without all of the colorful shotgun homes.

Chromatic Appeal

A trend in community-building is the worldwide chromatic homes movement that unites neighbors to renew, rebuild, and repurpose neighborhoods. A common thread among some of the most beloved places in the world is bright colors.

In the city of Burano, Italy, for example, homes feature one dominant color like pink, purple, yellow, or blue, and the colors alternate from house to house creating a streetscape so compelling that it draws tourists from around the world.

In the United States, bringing joyful color to historic places are the collections of wooden Victorian homes that feature a variety of colors on one home. Palettes of rich colors highlight decorative wood-work in intricate and unusual patterns so captivating that these homes have become known as "painted ladies." The conventional definition of "painted ladies"—Victorian houses built in San Francisco with three or more colors that embellish architectural details—has been in common parlance for a couple of decades (Pomada and Larsen; 1978, 1989, 1992). But missing has been the documentation of how other cities like Louisville, KY; Cincinnati, OH; New Albany, IN; Nashville, TN; Charleston, SC; as well as Eureka, CA have renewed neighborhoods by adopting the protocols of "painted ladies."

The original intention of this book was to make that case and put these other cities on the map of great places to see "painted ladies." We also wanted to show how this movement helped to "ignite these neighborhoods," thereby revitalizing these wonderful places that have existed for generations. But as we visited and consulted in other places, we learned that "painted ladies" did not just start in San Francisco in the 1960s, but have been around for hundreds of years in places like Havana, Cuba; Burano, Italy; Moscow, Russia; and Charleston, SC. We also noticed that colorful homes could have that "pop" factor with just one color and the appeal of joyful color was not limited to 100-year-old Victorians.

Michael Larsen, who with his co-author coined the term "painted ladies," encouraged me to develop a term with more utility that covers the scope of this book, becoming more flexible and expansive in usage. So it becomes "chromatic homes," which is not as sexy but provides the utility to describe this modern movement.

Perhaps defining chromatic homes and buildings is something like "in the eye of the beholder," or as the Supreme Court once defined pornography, *"I know it when I see it"* (Pomada and Larsen; 1978, 1989, 1992). It pops. In the words of a Nashville artist, *"it's a welcoming sign to the neighborhood."*

So why not broaden the definition of "painted ladies" well beyond its San Francisco residential roots, and evolve joyful color into new forms all over the world? Consider, for example, the evolution of rock and roll. It did not start and stop with the late Chuck Berry, but evolved into different forms, rhythms, and styles—pop, instrumental, progressive, and psychedelic rock, among others. Similarly, our intent is to acknowledge and honor the history of "painted ladies" while inspiring a chromatic grassroots movement to celebrate and spread joyful color to different structural styles, forms, and locations.

Why now?

Unfortunately, many cities and communities have missed their opportunity to regenerate these historic Victorian homes. Many, tragically, did not survive to see another century. Rather than focus only on the priceless but shrinking population of Victorian homes, why not leverage their "spirit" of color, renewal, and vibrancy? In this way, the "chromatic" building becomes an aggregating term that can apply to any structure embodying the chromatic homes' liveliness. It can be a home, a parking garage, a trailer, a centuries-old cathedral, or a restaurant, each structure sharing a colorful expression of beauty.

Can chromatic homes be the secret sauce for neighborhood and community regeneration?

Even in a city of too much sameness, it's possible to have an oasis of cool: well-preserved chromatic homes that can empower you to think big. Why not save a big, old, funky home that is ready for the wrecking ball? One simple trick is to turn the house into a beautiful chromatic home that might inspire the entire block of a neighborhood to do the same. It is important to understand what makes community possible and how community can lift our spirits. One of the most powerful arguments for renewing our neighborhoods comes from social critic Paul Goodman (1959: 17), who writes in his book *Growing Up Absurd*, *"A man has only one life and if during it he has no great environment, no community, he has been irreparably robbed of a human right."*

So, how do you make a great community? Housing is more than shelter. Entailing growth, support, nurture, and refuge, it is a symbol of who we are. New Urbanist planner Jan Gehl, in a YouTube lecture, captures this spirit by saying, *"Never ask what the city can do for your building, always ask what your building can do for the city."* Both Gehl and Goodman help set our compass for why and how to create a community that inspires human happiness.

Vibrant historic buildings are igniting neighborhoods everywhere, which is what this book is about: adding color to homes and buildings with love and care to create better neighborhoods and communities. As Donovan Rypkema, the world's leading historic preservationist states, *"It's about rebuilding communities in which people want to live."*

Activism

For some, this spirit of neighborhood activism began with Jane Jacobs. In her 1961 groundbreaking book, *The Life and Death of Great American Cities*, she shares the story of how she successfully fought against a freeway that was to be constructed through Greenwich Village in the late 1950s. Later, in the spring of 1970, the People's Park fight in Berkeley, CA inspired countless neighborhoods to create community through planning, architecture, diversity, health, color, and safety. Berkeley taught the world how to build sustainable and viable neighborhoods, a fact that is absent in most urban planning textbooks (Weinstein, 2008).

Activists also rose up to oppose war and to support the rights of minorities, the disabled, gay people, and senior citizens. At the same time, a growing movement demanded that Americans rethink the design of our cities to create livable, walkable communities of tolerance and diversity. Traditional planning ideas were turned upside-down. For example, the conventional wisdom in the real estate industry was that white houses have a better resale value than houses painted with flamboyant colors. This proved to be untrue.

"The urge to decorate and embellish one's dwelling is a common and primal force, evident even in the animal kingdom. For some people, though, it becomes an obsession, far out-stretching the simple shell-embellished seaside porch, or the witty garden gazebo. For some, a hobby or a digression develops into a life's work, a quest to leave a unique and undeniable mark on the world that reflects their own inner vision. An attempt to create a genuine alternative reality for themselves, their very own earthly paradise."

— Schaewen and Maizels (2000: 10)

The chromatic building challenges the dominant paradigm of modernism rooted in the work of French architect Le Corbusier, who took personalization out of architecture with "less is more." He turned buildings into non-human, faceless, repetitive designs without frills or nuance. The modernism of Le Corbusier became the standard design principle of the Soviet Union, Cuba, South America, and Central America. Taking out the frills and playfulness was cheaper. This regimented, machine-like sameness squelches the human spirit, belittling people into feeling powerless and ordinary. Today, in many cities around the world, such as Amsterdam, Havana, Moscow, and Paris, the most disreputable, crime-ridden buildings are these soulless barrack-style projects.

Similarly, in the United States, failures of large-scale public housing projects such as the Pruitt-Igoe in St. Louis, Missouri and Cabrini Green in Chicago, Illinois have been linked to Le Corbusier designs. However, not all modernism is a disaster if you consider postmodern designs like those in Amsterdam, The Hague, and Rotterdam, which use color and personalization on structures.

Scholarly research finds that ordinary and predictable streetscapes can produce boredom, sadness, and anxiety (Duany et. al, 2001; Speck, 2012; Montgomery, 2013). Conversely, research shows that an urban neighborhood filled with individual expression makes us happier and healthier (Montgomery, 2013). Socialism promotes equality that results in housing sameness with no differentiation from one unit to another. The only difference is the number on the door, which can be dehumanizing. And it is interesting to note that with the fall of the Soviet Union came an outburst of color and personalization on buildings in former socialist countries (Malakhov and Repina, 2014; Gilderbloom, 2018).

House-Self-Identity

The color, vibrancy, imagination, and creativity inherent in chromatic homes are expressions of self and community—colorful structural expressions that speak to the most precious part of what makes us human. Housing can be a symbol-of-self when homeowners, and sometimes renters, engage in home improvement projects.

"The house as symbol-of-self is deeply ingrained in the American ethos. The frontier image of the man clearing the land and building a cabin for himself and his family... to a culture inbred with this image, the house-self-identity is not far behind us" (Cooper, 1971: 12). Here, Cooper is paraphrasing psycho-analyst Carl Jung's view of one's home as closely tied to identity. This type of research is important. As President of the American Sociological Association, Louis Wirth in 1947 sought to promote *"housing as a field of research because we have the skills and insights."* Despite these pleas, research on housing and neighborhood dynamics has yet to be fully realized.

Art and Inspiration

Chromatic homes are often the choice of artists like painters, writers, and musicians who make their homes noticeable to the public as an expression of identity and often give birth to their art in unique and imaginative environments. In fact, artists are often among the first to occupy blighted urban neighborhoods, creating new facades and repurposing buildings, leading to regeneration with a chromatic tilt.

In San Francisco author Alice Walker, who wrote *The Color Purple*, occupied one of the most famous chromatic homes across from Alamo Square. Mark Twain wrote *Huckleberry Finn* and *The Adventures of Tom Sawyer* in a spectacular chromatic home in Hartford, Connecticut (Pomada and Larsen, 1992). He also wrote in a friend's "painted lady" in Hannibal, Missouri.

Lovability

Chromatic homes can make you feel good about yourself, they are relatively economical (as long as you can afford the paint), and their aesthetic value enhances neighborhood prosperity. Chromatic homes highlight the decorative artistry of each unique building, from banister to baluster, from dormer to door, from window to roofline.

Vibrant historic housing helps spark a neighborhood renaissance by making historic buildings lovable again. How many times have you heard, *I love this home, building, place,* or *neighborhood?* It comes from the heart. Creating a chromatic home transforms the ordinary, humdrum, and forgettable building into an extraordinary beauty that challenges conformity. Some people compare the allure of a brilliant chromatic home to the appeal of a rainbow in Waikiki that captures your eye, or to a red and gold cable car in San Francisco that touches your heart, or to the simple beauty of a blue and yellow Dutch tulip in full bloom that elicits a smile when you see it.

Like many of life's simple pleasures, chromatic homes bring joy to work or play in the home. They make the houses homes, turn them into cool places, transform neighborhoods, and make a city more lovable. Some also see chromatic homes as a reflection of sexual freedom/gay culture place-making. This is true of the three sister cities with the most remarkable chromatic homes: San Francisco, Miami, and New Orleans.

As Miami Beach resident, New Urbanist, and author Stephen Mouzon (2010: 199) says, *"If they can't be loved, they will not last. Any serious conversation about sustainable building must begin with the issue of lovability. If a building cannot be loved by those using and visiting it, then it is likely to be demolished and carted off to the landfill in only a generation or two, at which point its carbon footprint is meaningless. All of the embodied energy of its materials is lost (if they are not recycled.) All future energy savings are lost, too."*

Sustainability

A chromatic home is the economic magic bullet that renews a tired, old, cranky neighborhood. In the end, it is an expression of diversity—an essential characteristic of a healthy, evolving, and sustainable society. Donovan Rypkema states that every time one small building is demolished it is like wiping out the entire environmental benefit from the last 1,344,000 recycled aluminum cans. *"We've not only wasted an historic building, we've wasted months of diligent recycling by the good people of our community."* This is why preservationists view saving buildings as sustainable acts. It also explains why the greenest cities in the world like Amsterdam prohibit the demolition of any historic building, and if one is unintentionally destroyed by weather or catastrophe, 90% of the materials must be recycled.

Chromatic buildings can be the key to economic renewal in many neglected downtown neighborhoods, often anchoring revitalization efforts. These renovations generate higher property values for the owner and for the neighborhood. The Original Highlands in Louisville, which has the highest concentration of chromatic homes in Middle America, has seen the largest jump in property values of any neighborhood in the U.S. over the span of the last decade (UofL Center for Sustainable Urban Neighborhoods). This success should compel cities to encourage homeowners to paint drab houses with bright colors. Paint is probably the cheapest way to get "house proud." Chromatic buildings can be inexpensive and effective community economic development tools that do not require government funding, just sweat equity. These revived-by-colorful-paint houses renew abandoned neighborhoods; many become popular tourist destinations. (Photo on right: A senior citizen homeowner painted her house using sweat equity, and it only cost her $212 for eight cans of paint and brushes.) Some, however, oppose using chromatic buildings as a strategy for gentrification, claiming that such improvements push the poor out. Recent studies by Columbia University professor Lance Freeman show historic neighborhoods that invest in gentrification experience longer durations of occupancy by homeowners and tenants than in neighborhoods without such investment (Florida, 2002; Gilderbloom, 2019). Without gentrification, these areas typically continue to decline, with consequent abandoned property, increased crime, and substandard housing.

Sociology explains what happens in the neighborhood revitalization process, especially as it relates to the chromatic building. What happens when one's house influences changes in others?

As I show throughout this book, one home turned into a chromatic art piece can ignite other homes on the same street. Sociologists have found that when someone buys an organ for their home other neighbors buy organs as well; similarly, when someone installs a picket fence other neighbors are likely to do the same (Michelson, 1977). Or flip the script—someone fails to repair a broken window or stops mowing the lawn—it becomes a phenomenon that, if left unchecked, leads to neighborhood decline.

Diversity of color trumps the sameness of conformity in urban life. These are art pieces with attention-getting, playful, childlike colors that stand out and make you pause, smile, and chuckle. The chromatic home is outrageous, punk, gay, awful, and interesting, but never dull. The chromatic home makes a powerful statement that is inclusive and welcomes difference. We spend roughly half of our lives in our neighborhoods. Why not make them healthy, walkable, safe, prosperous, and just?

The chromatic home sends a message to the world that life is beautiful. These gussied up structures reflect happiness and tolerance for different lifestyles.

"We shape our buildings, afterwards, they shape us."

— Winston Churchill, October 28, 1944

San Francisco, California

Today, the largest collection of "painted ladies" in the world is in San Francisco—the first sister. The Chamber of Commerce claims these chromatic homes are one of the city's most popular tourist attractions; the "painted ladies" across from Alamo Square are the most photographed by tourists, ahead of such icons as the Golden Gate Bridge, cable cars, and Fisherman's Wharf. In the modern age, San Francisco's "painted ladies" sparked the worldwide movement to bring dynamic colors into neighborhoods of both the rich and the poor around the world (Pomada and Larsen; 1978, 1989, 1992).

These "painted ladies" are hallmarks of San Francisco's appeal and offer a valuable lesson in how to revitalize a failing neighborhood, turning "ugly" into "beautiful" with the artistic application of colorful paint. The modern day chromatic homes movement has its roots in the Psychedelic Era of the mid-1960s, igniting a spark that started a fire.

More than 100 years ago, nearly 48,000 modular Victorian houses were ordered out of catalogs, with parts pre-cut and put on wagons for mules to transport to neighborhoods, clubs, churches, and ethnic communities. Residents erected these houses. This community effort inspired the names of famous districts—Nob Hill, Chinatown, Mission District (mostly Hispanic), Little Russia, and North Beach (Little Italy). These districts were built between 1849 (Gold Rush) and 1915, with many surviving the earthquake of 1906. These homes expressed economic growth and individuality in bright colors: *red, yellow, chocolate, orange... everything that is loud is in fashion... stores are painted yellow or brown"* (California Architects and Builders News, April 1885; Pomada and Larsen, 1978).

During World Wars I and II, the "painted ladies" were painted a surplus battleship gray to camouflage them, as officials feared bombing. Randolph Delehanty (2000: 6) describes San Francisco at a cross-roads before the city's psychedelic music explosion started in 1967, *"I first came to San Francisco in the late 1960s during the heyday of Urban Renewal, when the city's Victorian houses were undervalued and under attack. I remember walking through the vacated blocks of the boarded-up West Addition, wondering at the madness of destroying this unique architectural ensemble and replacing it with sterile stucco buildings."* Eventually, a combination of neighborhood height limits, a resurgent Bay Area economy, and new people who saw old buildings in imaginative ways rescued the city's vintage houses. Today, it is almost impossible to find a shabby Victorian house in all of San Francisco.

Vivid colors also saved the cable cars in San Francisco. Shortly after World War II, there were calls to get rid of the cable car. Art Holmer and his brother Larry (a respected high-end furniture refinisher in San Francisco) were tasked by municipal government to paint the cable cars one last time. They disobeyed the order to paint the cars flat military green, instead using bright red, blue, yellow, and purple. According to the Cable Car Museum, Holmer also added expensive "gold leaf" paint to add a little more elogance. Ridership soared and Art Holmer became known as the "maestro" who saved the cable car.

Art Holmer's nephew, Rich Holmer, described the importance of his uncle's achievement of saving the now-iconic symbol of San Francisco. *"He was an interesting character and I always enjoyed talking with him at the end of the day at my Dad's furniture refinishing shop,"* said the younger Holmer. *"He was a true San Franciscan. Very little honor is given to the civil servants who contribute mightily to our cities and government institutions. People love to belittle bureaucrats and criticize them when their combined efforts are the basis of our democracy. Art deserves the recognition."*

Art Holmer's moving art of the colorful Cable Car helped inspire the chromatic homes movement.

A protest movement to save the cable car from extinction was galvanized by Art Holmer's changes. General Motors had succeeded, in other cities, in retiring rail and cable cars. But San Francisco beat back the car companies and won. Try to imagine San Francisco without the cable car. Tony Bennett would have had no song to sing, *Rice-a-Roni* would have needed a different icon, and green thinking on transportation would have no model.

Holmer inspired Victorian homeowners to paint colorful embellishments on their houses. During the Psychedelic Era in Haight-Ashbury, a rundown blue-collar neighborhood of colorless, manufactured Victorians, residents transformed their architecture with a spectrum of colors—bold, pastel, or earthy colors similar to those used by the Grateful Dead, Jefferson Airplane, Janis Joplin, Jimi Hendrix, and many other bands for light shows, posters, clothes, hair dye, tattoos, and cars (most notably, Janis Joplin's Porsche and John Lennon's Bentley).

Haight-Ashbury and other San Francisco Victorian neighborhoods were down-and-out, giving artists and musicians affordable spaces to create their art.

According to Randolph (2000), San Francisco wooden Victorian row houses proved to be surprisingly adaptable over time. Many have come full circle in their hundred-plus years from middle-class single-family houses, to being broken up into rooming houses or apartments, and back again to (very rich) single-family dwellings. The trend spread like wildfire. The famous neighborhood, Alamo Square, now known as "Postcard Row," is the most visited and photographed spot in San Francisco. This neighborhood of "painted ladies" has been in more than 70 films and numerous TV shows (Pomada and Larsen; 1978, 1989, 1992).

Ten years after the cable car was saved from extinction, the Psychedelic Era in San Francisco gave birth to the "painted lady." Street art also bloomed in down-and-out neighborhoods, where gingerbread-style Victorians stood neglected. Other California cities emulated this trend—the seaside towns of Capitola, Santa Barbara, Venice, Santa Monica, and Santa Cruz, along with San Francisco Bay cities of Oakland and Berkeley.

Chromatic Homes: The Joy of Color in Historic Places

"Each city has its own fingerprint of style and story. However, here in The Mission, in San Francisco, I see a level of CULTURA that inspires the world."

— Carlos Santana

Miami, Florida

The second sister city of chromatic homes is the Art Deco Historic District in South Miami Beach, built in the 1920s and 1930s as a modern take on classical and Mediterranean resort architecture. The area flourished at first, but neglect soon set in, and by the 1960s and 1970s had become run-down, boarded-up, and abandoned. A woman named Barbara Capitman, the Jane Jacobs of the South, fought developers and elected leaders who wanted to level the dilapidated Art Deco buildings and replace them with glass high-rises and condos. She sparked a relentless battle to preserve these one-of-a-kind buildings.

Capitman, leading a small group of preservationists starting in 1976, made enough noise to stop the developers. And within three years, a one-square-mile area, known as South Beach, was listed on the National Register of Historic Places—the only place to get such a designation in the 20th century. Her small group of preservationists saved the district, protecting these historic structures with code regulations and designating each structure with Art Deco pastel color markers.

South Beach in Miami has the largest concentration of Art Deco buildings in the world. Ironically, the charismatic leader of this movement to save South Beach was later kicked out of the group she founded because of her refusal to compromise on historic preservation.

Like San Francisco, Miami Beach is a fine example of the preservation practice of using paint to highlight architectural details.

Miami Beach resident and author Stephen Mouzon (2010: 199, 210) says in his insightful book that people don't destroy beautiful historic architecture and, *"If a building cannot be loved, it will not last... it is a sensual delight."* This is why Art Deco will be with us forever. Curves and colors have been repurposed from the original Art Deco design in Western Europe reflecting a Caribbean salsa flavor.

Today, the Art Deco district of South Beach is the number one tourist destination in Miami. The occupants are a diverse group of architects, painters, models, designers, artists, and musicians.

In South Beach, ordinary people defeated real estate developers who wanted to tear down old structures, in part, by painting the buildings pastel Art Deco colors and pushing for tougher preservation codes.

Today, these properties are untouchable.

New Orleans, Louisiana

The third sister of the chromatic homes triptych is New Orleans—where street after street of shotgun homes were saved and renewed with colorful paint. According to urban studies researcher and writer, Carrie Beth Lasley, PhD, *"...in NOLA, a brightly painted house is the standard."* The culture is so deeply tied to French Caribbean that it is standard to add color, and the earliest settled are among the most colorful. Places like Mid-City are full of colorful historic homes—not modern design—but it is still mostly vernacular in design and relatively old (Gilderbloom, 2008).

Tourists love the color and diversity of New Orleans. Notice that the chromatic homes of New Orleans have their own unique style that reflects racial and cultural diversity (Fitzpatrick, 2006).

These beloved shotguns would be gone if not for a powerful preservation group, Preservation Resources Center, organized by hundreds of volunteers to save, paint, and renovate these homes, which are now occupied by a diverse group that includes black, gay, white, Cajun, and elderly people. Contrary to the gentrification caused by chromatic homes in San Francisco's Mission and Fillmore Districts, a large number of these homes are still occupied by middle- and low-income people (Gilderbloom, 2008).

After Hurricane Katrina, developers called for the demolishing of many chromatic homes in some low-income neighborhoods in New Orleans, but the residents fought back and were able to save many of them. They remain desirable, for affordability and popularity among tourists, planners, and residents (Gilderbloom, 2008). These chromatic homes have withstood major hurricanes, including Katrina, which caused more than 1,200 deaths, and have been resilient against the federal highway department's destructive planning practices that promote sprawl, freeways, and dissected downtowns.

Cincinnati, Ohio

An inspiring rebirth of a black neighborhood can be found in Cincinnati's Findlay Market, which expands to the larger Over-the-Rhine area near downtown Cincinnati. Previously, this area was known for danger, violence, boarded-up buildings, foreclosures, abandonments, graffiti, and open drug trade. Today, the Findlay Market is the "go-to" farmers' market that brings shoppers from a 100-mile radius and is a popular magnet for tourists.

Historic Findlay Market used bright colors to revitalize homes in an area that was once 90% vacant and one of the most dangerous neighborhoods in the nation. This revitalization was aided by a 3.6-mile surface rail loop connector, which stimulated investments estimated at $1.4 billion in new development on vacant and dilapidated properties along its route, followed by startup restaurants, farmers' markets, and other establishments.

Bright paint covers the angry graffiti that once dominated the area, lifting neighborhood self-esteem.

Columbia Tusculum is a small enclave of chromatic homes that was Cincinnati's first settlement. It is protected by local preservation ordinances and includes a colorful array of structures. Residents are proud of its standing as the largest neighborhood of chromatic homes in Ohio. Most of the Victorians were built between 1849 and 1915, consequent to the introduction of the car. Eighteen buildings have been placed on the National Register of Historic Places. Again, emerging from the 1960s were the "urban pioneers" in the 1970s and 1980s, inspired by San Francisco's "painted ladies." They started a movement to paint these homes in colorful ways.

These chromatic homes have attracted new investments for home construction and at least fifteen startups. The Victorians are on narrow lots with front porches near the sidewalk, which create a greater community feeling, with low crime rates and increased property values; many houses now sell for $300,000 or more.

Covington, Kentucky

Across the Ohio River, award-winning preservationists Emily Wolff and Paul Weckman have single-handedly regenerated MainStrasse Village, a historic German neighborhood in Covington, Kentucky. They renovated several buildings, turning two of them—Otto's and Frida 602—into 4-star restaurants. They have renovated 100-year-old buildings in the neighborhood including one that is 160 years old. Today, this area of colorful buildings has sparked pride and prosperity for Covington's historic downtown neighborhood, which was once abandoned and neglected. Emily reflects on their journey:

"Otto's was definitely the project that sparked change not only for the historic downtown, but also for Paul and I as community developers. It ignited a passion for preservation and growing community. We bought the brick three-story building in 2002 for $210,000 with the help of our parents. Paul and I were expecting twins, and the building provided us a location for both our home and our business. Paul was the chef, janitor, and dishwasher, and I (Emily) was the interior and exterior designer and painter, host, and waiter! We lived above the restaurant until 2010, when we moved our growing family to the former Saint Aloysius Rectory around the corner. Now all three floors of 521 Main Street are utilized for Otto's. This building is currently worth $500,000.

"The Rectory was our first major renovation project. We purchased the building for $150,000 (with no plumbing, electric, doors, or windows) and it would now list for about $750,000. These price increases are directly correlated to the investment in historic redevelopment, the adaptive reuse of forgotten, old buildings, bold paint colors on our restaurants, and the general belief in rebuilding a community.

"Paul and I have restored dozens of properties in our Village. Our current residential focus is what we are calling the 9th Street Redevelopment Plan. In 2015, 9th Street was experiencing major decline due to slum/abandoned properties and the increase of heroin and prostitution. We decided the only way to make a positive change was to invest in some of the worst properties in our community. We purchased our first 9th Street property for $16,000. It was in terrible shape, ready for demolition, and there was a drive-by shooting on the night of our closing. Paul and I went all in on the project and we sold the building for $320,000 in 2016, and it sold again for $410,000 in the summer of 2017. We have five other projects slated for 9th Street.

"As for commercial preservation and redevelopment, Project 602, which is now home to Frida 602, has received much attention as a business catalyst for the neighborhood. We not only saved a pre-civil war building on the brink of collapse, but we provided a beautiful and viable building on the corner of our Main Street business district, and added over 30 jobs to our local economy.

"Painting the businesses and apartment buildings in bright, colorful tones was like a message to folks that Covington is coming back. Today, we employ in our restaurants and renovation projects nearly 100 people. We not only have a love for preservation, but for cornerstone projects.

"Paul and I love identifying the need for preservation and taking action. Whether it be preserving buildings, structures, connections, or community, it all has a place in the neighborhood stabilization process. We have another great corner project on the horizon in 2018. Furthermore, I have also been focusing on neighborhood parks as well as the use of public art to connect communities—making the space safe and inviting to pedestrians."

Chromatic Homes: The Joy of Color in Historic Places

Portland, Oregon

In 1999, Jay Hornstein and Todd Dugan were working as waiters. In love and tired of renting, they dreamed of a cool San Francisco-style "painted lady" to call home. They began searching for the *"worst possible house in a nice neighborhood,"* but that initial house hunting netted zero results. So, Jay and Todd recalibrated and ultimately purchased *"the worst house on the street, in the worst neighborhood."*

Their month-long search yielded a home with an asking price of $109,000, but they paid $115,000 due to other bidders. With over a century of remodels and neglect, it was a real eyesore. While replacing a porch light, they discovered the shingles covering the structure were hiding an 1892 Queen Anne Stick style Victorian that was originally painted yellow and blue over a hundred years ago. Thus began their restoration adventure. They could not afford to hire folks, so they took the standard sweat equity route. In Jay's words, *"You need a sense of humor... it took five dumpsters, but it was a joy."*

"We discovered it had pocket doors that were covered up."

The exterior took two years to complete with approximately four months dedicated to painting. Todd took the lead on the structural repairs, and with a 2 ½-inch brush and a 4-inch brush, Jay began painting a masterpiece.

Together, they selected a beautiful palette of colors, yet quite by accident, the paint colors were not mixed correctly, yielding some truly unique combinations.

As fate would have it, however, the color combinations still worked, adding yet another dimension of character and appeal. Their house went from the worst-looking house on the street to the best-looking home in the neighborhood.

What did the overall investment and return picture look like for Jay and Todd? The cost of the satin paint was $1,000 with another $500 for caulk, sandpaper, tools, brushes, scaffolding, and ground cover. The first and second stories of the house received two coats of paint, with one coat for the third floor. Altogether, they invested $25,000 to $30,000 and found adventurous joy and creativity together as a couple. They ultimately lifted the spirits of the neighborhood.

In 2007, their home sold for $389,000. The new buyers chose to paint it black with a thin yellow stripe around it, and the value of the house plummeted.

"Buildings help define a culture, architecture should be a humanizing force, and a well-built community can foster a well-lived life."

— Vincent Scully

Nashville, Tennessee

Think of this home as a piece of public art that is regenerating the neighborhood. As the owner Lesley Patterson-Marx states, *"it's a place that breaks the rules of the neighborhood by putting a painting on the house that is welcoming, joyful, and reflects Buddhist and Dutch traditions."* She, along with her husband and child, turned this banal home into a gem. Lesley loves it when people stroll by and commend her home as a piece of art that makes the neighborhood "nicer" and "cool." She says she wouldn't sell her home even if offered half a million dollars! Lesley Patterson-Marx calls it a shield that protects the neighborhood from developers who are eager to demolish her home and build expensive condos. Her painted home is an expression of her values.

The painter of this chromatic design was Scott Guion with Cajun roots who was paid $1,000. He is redefining this South Nashville neighborhood, and is having an even bigger impact in nearby Berry Hill, Tennessee by painting colorful murals on fences and houses.

The modern chromatic homes movement was inspired by San Francisco in the sixties, but in the next section of this book we show that such homes go back hundreds of years, even to the 1600s.

Russia: Moscow, Saint Petersburg, and Samara

The oldest and perhaps most beautiful chromatic building in the world is Saint Basil's Cathedral, the 16th-century structure that occupies Red Square. It has become a symbol of Russia. The church was built in 1555, but the current color scheme was developed between 1680 and 1848. The onion domes, originally gold, were painted multiple colors in the 19th century. The use of color goes back hundreds of years.

The cathedral is Baroque and Neoclassical, and is an expression of romantic nationalism. Stalin wanted the church destroyed so military tanks could come into Red Square, but religious leaders, preservationists, university students, and ordinary people resisted, preserving this iconic structure for generations to come. The building was secularized by the Communists in 1928 and was a popular museum.

Once again, this magnificent church inspires awe; there is no other church with more visual spellbinding power. This structure was so admired that it was duplicated. Another Russian cathedral preserved for posterity is St. Petersburg's Savior of the Blood—named in honor of Alexander II, who was killed by an assassin's bomb at the site in 1881.

A chromatic home symbolizes hope, pride, community investment, renewal, and regeneration. It was a break from the conformity dictated by Communism. During the fall of the Soviet Union, the chromatic homes movement was reignited throughout the Soviet bloc in Ukraine, Budapest, Poland, and Russia. Many of the austere modernist Le Corbusier-inspired buildings were painted bright colors. As Harvey Molotch noted in his book, *It cues in that someone of responsibility and concern is around. Color, and its maintenance, can thus be an urban force for confidence.*

With the fall of the authoritarian Soviet state came an outpouring of neighborhood empowerment movements. One example is in Samara, Russia, a 16-hour drive from Moscow. There, the "Tom Sawyer volunteers" fix up dilapidated, century-old houses by painting them multiple colors, and in this way, these volunteers create community pride. Led by university professors at Samara University (Sergei Malakhov and Evgenia Repina, 2014), these volunteers have renovated abandoned homes and buildings. Like Tom Sawyer, the fictional character who persuaded others to paint a fence, they have attracted between 20 to 30 volunteers, and their collective efforts have resulted in what is now a "free space" for alternative lifestyles. As reflected in these photos, the "Tom Sawyer" volunteer effort has been a success. This approach can also be found in New Orleans, where the work of hundreds of volunteers is coordinated by the Preservation Resource Center.

Neighborhoods in Cuba

Cuba is known for having the world's largest collection of intact Spanish colonial architecture. The bright pastel colors are in the harbor area near massive, moated stone fortresses created 400 years ago. Blue, yellow, green, and turquoise pastels are the dominant colors, as documented by archaeologists, who use microscopes to determine original colors. Structures are then repainted in those colors. These authentic and historic preservation practices create a harbor area that is dramatic and awe-inspiring. Today, Havana has become a top tourist destination, bringing in an infusion of cash that helps prevent the collapse of socialist Cuba's economy.

The Cuban government, following the collapse of the Soviet Union, has had to find new forms of economic development. Historic preservation has been the linchpin of these efforts, allowing buildings to be renovated instead of demolished. City planners and architects, including this book's author, have been invited to help with Cuba's post-Soviet renewal. Successful neighborhood renewals were led by abstract "Santeria" painters and artists, whose eye-popping creations attract tourists, and two neighborhoods in Havana have renovated the homely Le Corbusier structures with spectacular colors.

In Hamel Alley, Salvador Gonzalez Escalona's creation reinvents the drab concrete and steel with a canvas of color and ornamentation that is provocative, challenging, unique, and often hostile toward the repressive socialist system. Salvador calls the Cuban government "racist" because it prevents official government tourist groups from visiting. This area was considered one of the poorest and most violent neighborhoods in Havana. His artistic creations, however, have been successful indications of how art and color can dramatically change a neighborhood while increasing jobs, shopping, and pride-of-place.

Salvador hopes to expand beyond Hamel Alley and revitalize the nearby Cayo Hueso community, a few blocks away from University of Havana. The Cuban tourist industry does not promote this destination. Salvador's work highlights government oppressions. His art and vibrant mosaic monuments are inspired by John Chamberlain of New York and are a celebration of Afro-Cuban culture.

José Fuster's Santeria-inspired art in Western Havana focuses on sexual liberation, domination, and repression, and has had a dramatic impact on the transformation of 78 pre-Castro modern flat concrete homes (Fuster, 2016). Fuster's work with broken tile is influenced by Antoni Gaudi in Barcelona, but with a Cuban aesthetic emphasizing God, sex, and beauty.

As with the artist Salvador, Cuban officials discourage tourism to this transformed neighborhood. As expected, the government efforts to discourage tourism have had the reverse effect, making tourists curious. Tourists appreciate the area for its entrepreneurial spirit, where artists working from home sell original artwork. Tourism created by chromatic homes generates jobs.

These Cuban homes are evidence of the movement's growth.

Burano, Italy

One of the most beautiful and captivating neighborhoods painted in an array of colors can be found in Burano, Italy, which is where Michelangelo purchased lace. Hundreds of years ago, the local fishermen had the buildings painted in bright pastel colors so they could find their docks. This fishing village, a 30-minute boat ride from Venice, is now one of the top tourist destinations in Italy.

Travel writer Suzy Strutner (2013) rhapsodizes about the emotional impact of Burano, calling it the *"cheeriest little island that will lift you... if you're in need of an emotional boost... its colors pop and sizzle."* But residents of Burano cannot paint their homes just any color; the state government dictates house colors. The result is a community so vivid that it inspires everyone who experiences its charm.

The power of chromatic homes sustains neighborhoods, creating glee, pride, hope, prosperity, and community. History is preserved; tourism provides enough prosperity so that the "little people" who have lived here for many generations are not displaced. They prosper with their tiny shops of art, jewelry, photographs, and dining. It's an island of prosperity and sustainability.

Chromatic Homes: The Joy of Color in Historic Places

Amsterdam, Netherlands

These brick four- and five-story warehouses were built during a period of unprecedented prosperity between 1600 and 1670. The black color on the bricks was tar, which sealed the building from cold and rain to protect stored goods. The red and green shutter doors were installed to add a strong contrast. Today, the wealthy class in Amsterdam clamors for these historic warehouse structures.

Rembrandt's 17th-century factory sits in the center of Amsterdam, with the original green shutters still intact, and some red highlights against traditional Dutch brown stone facade. Below is the modern chromatic look of buildings in Amsterdam and Rotterdam that brightens up the common historic structures, which are typically brown stone and brick. The famous post-modern yellow Cube House in Rotterdam is a remarkable building that is like no other residential building in the world.

Arles, France: "Yellow House (The Street)"

Van Gogh famously painted the work known as "Yellow House (The Street)" in Arles, France, in late 1888. If you look closely at the painting below, you can see emerald green, sea foam green, turquoise, pink, brown, violet, burnt orange, mauve, terracotta orange, pale yellow, gold, black, and indigo. The sky is a midnight blue. Van Gogh's painting was not a realistic portrayal, but was embellished with a variety of colors. Arles did not have the wealth to put multiple colors on buildings, but Van Gogh was imagining how it could look with the introduction of colors. Artists often take liberties with literal truth to create beauty. (Photo on right: A painter reimagining plain buildings in Corfu, Greece with a variety of colors. In reality, there was only one basic color. We suspect this embellishment was similar to Van Gogh's "Yellow House.")

Louisville Love Story:
How One City Turned Around A Dying Neighborhood

One of Louisville's greatest assets—and best kept secrets—is the city's collection of preserved 100-year-old Victorian houses painted in three or more colors.

Louisville ranks fourth nationally, and The Original Highlands now has the highest concentration of "painted ladies" in Kentucky. It's official, Louisville joins San Francisco, Miami, and New Orleans as the fourth of the chromatic home sister cities, followed by Cincinnati as the newly adopted fifth sister.

On streets such as Edward, Morton, Highland, Hepburn, Rubel, Breckinridge, Christy, Barrett, and Bardstown, visitors can stroll through many antique shops, art galleries, record/CD shops, book stores, and lots of fabulous restaurants and bars late into the evening. It is a diverse economic mixture of millionaires and blue/pink collar workers living side by side in mansions and shotgun houses.

This was not always the case in Louisville. In 1992, *America's Painted Ladies: The Ultimate Celebration of Our Victorians* (Pomada and Larsen, 1992) listed only one house that was significant in Louisville among its 375 pages—126 Pope Street in the Clifton neighborhood. According to Debra Harlan, a preservationist who worked for the city, Louisville had only one "painted lady" until 1995, when Victorians began to be painted with three or more shades.

But the presence of chromatic neighborhoods has been ignored by many.

The Princeton Press published *Louisville Guide*, a book with 449 pages with black and white photos of historic and modern homes, but without photos of "painted ladies" (Luhan, Domer, & Mohney, 2004). Nor does the popular textbook *Historic Preservation* by Norman Tyler (2000) mention "painted ladies" as a preservation technique. And Lisa Westmoreland-Doherty (2008) fails to celebrate the role of chromatic homes in her survey of Louisville, Kentucky neighborhoods.

The best books on Louisville architecture are by Steve Wiser, who has written on modern, historic, and carriage houses, but not about chromatic homes in Louisville. What stands out about Wiser's works, compared to the others, is that he uses color photographs, where as the other books rely on black and white pictures. Today, however, sparkling and vibrant chromatic homes are popping up at an increasing rate throughout the Louisville metro area.

Brightly colored houses are not always popular with the officials who set codes and regulations. Some cities try to ban chromatic homes. Preservationists argue the colors are historically inaccurate. People file lawsuits and harass homeowners whose house ornamentation, they say, crosses the threshold of "acceptability and prudence." Yet, other cities have made bright colors mandatory, as in the cities of Capitola, California and Burano, Italy.

Paint or no paint?

In Old Louisville, considered a gem by preservation experts, local government prohibits painting over brick, which is wise for maintenance purposes and why people prefer brick. If your house has been painted already you can paint it again, but it needs to be an approved historic color, or they issue a stop work order and sometimes require the owner to paint it again. In these cases, perhaps it's in the area's best interest to allow the owner to repaint it without intervention.

"It's been said that at its best, preservation engages the past in a conversation with the present over a mutual concern for the future."

— William Murtagh, first "Keeper" of the National Register of Historic Places

Some preservation boards will dictate which colors can be used. In many cases they mandate "earth colors" with dark browns, grays, and greens that are often ahistorical. Archeologists and newspaper accounts tell us that there was a variety of bright colors going back one hundred years in San Francisco, and as much as four hundred years in the Netherlands, Italy, and Cuba.

Ten years ago, we wrote a report for Preservation Kentucky noting the success of a program for small Kentucky towns called *"Let's Paint the Town."* The program was a success and revitalized many small, rural downtowns and made them inviting places. The state government supplied paint to renew storefronts, and provided consultants to advise appropriate paint colors.

Preservation movements are vital, yet at times may seem oppressive, when an unelected, appointed body makes decisions on "appropriate" historic color. For example, a strict preservation ordinance in The Original Highlands lost when residents were informed an appointed board could require earth tone colors. Richard Jett, former head of Louisville Preservation said this was a false argument designed to defeat a preservation ordinance in The Original Highlands. Under those circumstances, many of the chromatic homes in this book would not have existed. The "earth color" urban legend hurts the preservation movement. Moreover, prohibitions on painting brick should also be lifted to let the homeowner decide, not government.

Vinyl Siding

Where government should get involved is with vinyl siding being used on housing, which hurts the house and the neighborhood. Vinyl siding is seen more in the poorest neighborhoods of Louisville and it signals distress and lack of investment. Government should prohibit the ugly brown and gray vinyl siding that is used on manufactured housing in preservation districts. Vinyl siding causes a decline in value of the house and it stops homeowners from trying to paint another color.

The movement for vinyl siding began in 1992. The product is often covered with pollution, mold, or toxins from industrial pollutants that are hard to remove. Houses covered in vinyl siding look dirty after about 10 years. It cheapens it and looks like manufactured housing. Valuation goes down for the vinyl house and might even bring down the value of houses next door—just the opposite of what a chromatic home can do.

Mouzon (2010: 227) argues putting vinyl over historic wood is one of the worst things you can do to a historic structure: *"You vinylized your Victorian, covering up all the wood siding with vinyl, and clapping vinyl panels all over your gingerbread and trim work. Behind the vinyl you may now be collecting moisture and deteriorating the woodwork so that when your kids or some other future resident decides to undo the damage you have done, they're likely to find a rotten mess when they remove the vinyl."*

In fact, Louisville's Habitat for Humanity does not allow any of its housing to use vinyl siding. Instead, they insist on using "Hardie board" fiber cement siding with a wood grain and smooth classic look that lasts longer and can come either pre-painted in bright colors or ready for painting. Habitat for Humanity is also replacing vinyl siding on houses when the occupant moves out because of death, hospitalization, or the desire to leave. It's not expensive to replace vinyl siding with wood or Hardie board, especially if you use your own sweat equity and simply take off the plastic, remove the rotten pieces, and replace with wood followed by sanding and a good paint job.

Louisville's Habitat officials estimate it costs about $3,000 to replace vinyl siding with Hardie board with 1,200 square feet for materials. Habitat for Humanity's "Restore" can also provide a variety of paints at a bargain price. San Francisco and Miami's South Beach prevent this cheap and unattractive vinyl housing from being put over original wood, stone, or brick.

A Historic Look at Victorians in The Original Highlands

Victorians in The Originals Highlands date back to the late 1800s. Donkeys pulled in pre-cut modular crafted wood that was unique in style from other nearby cities like New Albany, IN; Covington, KY; Newport, KY; and Cincinnti, OH. They used redwood trees in San Francisco, and in Louisville they used pine and oak from nearby forests as well as recycled wood from nearby abandoned steamships that had to end their journeys at the Falls of the Ohio. In fact, many of the Victorians along Morton Avenue in The Original Highlands added a 12-foot by 11-foot third-floor observation deck. This unintended benefit of the third-floor addition was that it helped to cool the house on hot summer days. These homes on Morton Avenue are known as "steamboat Victorians."

These beautiful Victorians were assembled by hand, without electric hammers, saws, or drills. Unlike wealthier neighborhoods, whose homes signaled their social status with strong masculine stone and brick (mini castles), the houses in Louisville's Original Highlands were mostly made of wood by the growing middle class of teachers, nurses, bookkeepers, lawyers, and shop owners who lived above the grocery stores and pharmacies. The craftsmanship was amazing and is too expensive to replicate today. The upwardly mobile middle class would turn horse stables into carriage houses as a common feature (Wiser, 2016). Today, this neighborhood remains a classic walkable neighborhood that New Urbanists prescribe for our urban fabric—grocery stores, pharmacies, and pubs (Speck, 2010; Duany et al., 2001).

The Original Highlands was the first ring suburb east of Louisville. Toilets were outside the home, heat was made by burning coal and wood in fireplaces, and houses were cooled by high ceilings that allowed hot air to rise and to be released by the transom windows and unused third-floor attics. Louisville was once known for its shroud of dirty air hanging over the city in winter, with smoke from factories and fireplaces. Horse droppings covered the streets, creating health hazards.

Electricity and cars became increasingly available in Louisville around 1915. Fans were installed, bikes and horses were parked outside, and people walked to the store, church, school, and work. This is how your (great) grandmother might have lived: no appliances, cable, Wi-Fi, CNN, central air, iPhone, nor even large closets, considering that most citizens of those days had only two changes of clothes. The average bedroom was too small to accommodate a king-sized bed, and two separate twin beds were the norm for a married couple. Moreover, the mixture of housing types and sizes allowed people with a range of incomes to live on the same block. Rufer Avenue, for example, was a street occupied by descendants of slaves. These neighborhoods were economically and racially integrated.

Like many other historic downtown neighborhoods, abandonment became a major problem in the 1970s and 1980s. Neighbors recall a place of high crime, open prostitution (with red lights in the windows of buildings along Baxter Avenue), drugs, biker gangs, harassment of gay people and minorities, halfway houses, and boarded-up buildings. You could buy Victorian houses for as little as $36,000 in 1988.

Today, Louisville's Original Highlands is one of America's greatest comeback stories, and it represents the future of how people should live in an era of climate change: dense, mixed-income, walkable, close to stores for everyday needs, places of worship, and lots of edgy shops pushing the envelope. Residents of The Original Highlands prefer to live in an environmentally friendly manner, near their workplace, recreation, museums, theaters, and school, by living in smaller spaces, by walking and riding bikes, and by taking a bus instead of relying exclusively on a car.

Many of these residents want to reduce their carbon footprint. They want to live in a manner that supports carbon reduction strategies.

National surveys by Wakefield and Kaufman call The Original Highlands one of America's "coolest neighborhoods," based on *Hip-O-Meter*, which evaluates a location's architecture, livability, retail, demographics, restaurants, nightspots, gay-friendliness, and unconventionality. The New Urbanism movement praises the healthy walkability of the place. This area also has a heavy concentration of Airbnb listings; a good portion of these Airbnb profits are used to improve Victorians with new paint, landscaping, and energy-saving devices.

Other neighborhoods joining The Original Highlands include Sunset Park, NYC; Over-the-Rhine in Cincinnati, OH (also featured in this book); and Elgin, IL. *Fodors Travel Guide* also calls The Original Highlands a must-see neighborhood when traveling in Kentucky. And some believe the success began with chromatic homes! Montgomery (2013) finds that environmental stimulation in an urban neighborhood is what makes residents happier than those in traditional suburban neighborhoods.

The Original Highlands neighborhood has for decades attracted artists, musicians, writers, and other creatives to the Bohemian way of life, which emanates outward from its funky but chic main thoroughfare, Bardstown Road. This area is notable for being the home of the late, legendary gonzo journalist, Hunter S. Thompson. The indie rock band, My Morning Jacket, recorded one of their hit albums in The Original Highlands. Tom Cruise once lived there, and even Senator Mitch McConnell is a resident.

This neighborhood is an excellent example of the reasons why people choose to own, fix, and paint a Victorian-era home in disrepair. First, they can express their personal styles. Second, there is a chance for profitable returns on investment. A two-and-a-half story Victorian provides bonus rooms on the third floor, which can be converted to an apartment, increasing the square footage while using modern energy-saving techniques of insulation and venting, and passive solar electricity. A 2,000-square-foot home can be profitably expanded by opening up the attic, turning an unused carriage house into a home, or by a converting a basement into a studio. While some of these units are illegal, officials seem to look the other way and don't enforce codes that mandate only two generations of family members.

Chromatic homes are often located in 100-year-old historic neighborhoods with slow two-way streets, bike lanes, a large stock of wooden (not brick or stone) housing, affordable prices for the working class, and friendliness to preservation activity. Ideally, these neighborhoods have a good tree canopy and sidewalks that encourage walking, with a good Walk Score. In addition, there are dog parks, active neighborhood associations, affordable homeownership opportunities, and diversity.

Many of the original Victorian structures are now small business startups, antique stores, consignment shops, pubs, bookstores, record stores, tattoo parlors, hair salons, sports bars, and high-end restaurants. (A survey by my graduate students found that eight out of the top ten restaurants in Louisville are in historic buildings that were renovated.) These places serve as magnets for tourists, homebuyers, and renters. In The Original Highlands, up to 50,000 people can come to Halloween parades, St. Patrick's Day parades, community fairs, sporting events, zombie walks, fundraising marathons, and, of course, a nightlife in the many restaurants and pubs that cater to straight and gay.

These neighborhoods are improved by people who take risks. They renovate homes and reclaim space while creating prosperity for themselves and neighbors. Recently, the Property Value Assessor's Office in Jefferson County, KY found that The Original Highlands has the lowest amount of foreclosures along with the highest appreciation rates compared to 178 other neighborhoods. Colorful paint leads to revitilization, renovation, new construction, well-paying jobs, and prosperity. Notably, the Kentucky State Data Center in 2015 found no displacement of the population by race or income. This is contrary to critics' claims that investment in poor neighborhoods results in displacement of the poor. In fact, there has been a small increase in the number of black, Asian, and Hispanic people, along with a substantial increase in gay homeowners and gay-owned businesses in The Original Highlands. Moreover, five homeless shelters are located here.

Contrary to the claims of anti-gentrification activists, this neighborhood has seen one of the largest spikes of newly built rental housing in Louisville, with 398 new units priced as low as $850 for studios and $950 for one-bedrooms. Another 450 affordable units are planned in 2019 to 2021 on the western edge of The Original Highlands. Many traditional single-family homes are converted into two-, three-, or four-unit homes. Perhaps the presence of chromatic homes is a symbol of tolerance and diversity.

A larger number of preserved older homes in urban neighborhoods leads to lower rents and home prices (Gilderbloom, 2008). Investment creates a healthier, safer, and more prosperous neighborhood that is better for all residents. Savvy investors also recognize that the neighborhoods with the highest return on housing investment are in Victorian neighborhoods.

Sam Watkins, former director of the Louisville Central Community Center, told a crowd of community leaders, *"There is nothing wrong with black people making profit in the renewal of inner city neighborhoods. Grow up!"* Watkins, along with the UofL Center for Sustainable Urban Neighborhoods and the City of Louisville, turned the city's most dangerous neighborhood, East Russell, into a safe, vibrant, mixed-income, and proud community that has won acclaim from Martin Luther King III (Gilderbloom; 2008, 2019).

"Therefore, when we build, let us think we build forever. Let it not be for present delight, nor for present use alone; let it be work that our descendants will thank us for."

— John Ruskin (Tyler, 2000)

Graffiti and Angry Art: Detroit, Houston, and Louisville

Not every chromatic home ignites or regenerates a neighborhood, and there are failures in nearly every city. MacArthur Genius Grant winner Rick Lowe was famous for his shotgun home project in Houston, Texas, which was hailed as a great way to reclaim the abandoned and deteriorating homes in poor neighborhoods. It was given a given thumbs-up by the mayor's task force on Houston housing (Gilderbloom, 2007). Unfortunately, the project did not spark regeneration and most of the chromatic homes have been painted white, covering protest art such as, *"What Washington needs is adult supervision."* There were a few good designs, but they were negated by bad graffiti-like designs.

Not all expressions of color are joyful. Houses covered with graffiti-like designs are an urban eyesore that devalues neighborhoods. Do you think a bank is going to loan money on a house across the street from one of these graffiti homes? On the adjacent page is a once great Detroit home that symbolizes chaos, confusion, and conflict. Louisville hired unemployed youth to paint over boarded-up windows and doors in hundreds of abandoned homes in West Louisville. It was a disaster for neighborhoods trying to regenerate themselves. Outraged neighborhood council representatives argued it made neighborhoods worse, not better, and demanded that the program be ended.

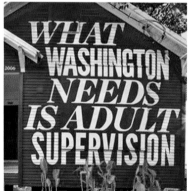

Regeneration has not happened in every downtown neighborhood in Louisville either. West Louisville provides a case in point, as it was built around the same time as The Original Highlands, with many of the same architects and builders. West Louisville has lost 5,500 historic structures, according to the mayor's office. Segregated neighborhoods declined rapidly due to a lack of significant investment in infrastructure and poor environmental quality.

There are many causes for this: lack of civic associations, toxic industries nearby, food deserts, limited shopping choices, low rates of homeownership, higher than average interest rates, and an absence of chromatic homes. Moreover, heavy concentrations of halfway houses, drug and alcohol rehab programs, liquor stores, rentals, pawn shops, prostitution, fencing operations, gang activity, and drugs cause neighborhood abandonment and fuel violent crime. Insurance rates for cars and homes are also high in these areas, and investors are less likely to buy in neighborhoods where they are unlikely to profit.

These "lost neighborhoods" can be saved with common sense green planning practices, capable leadership, community associations, and preservation practices. They need investment, not disinvestment.

I discuss these factors in my next book, *"Ten Commandments of Livable Neighborhoods: Creating Healthy, Safe, Prosperous, Just, and Sustainable Neighborhoods"* (Gilderbloom, 2019). Oddly, a local government program in Louisville went awry by hiring unemployed, disadvantaged youth to paint messages of pride, art, and empowerment on the plywood of these boarded up windows (see opposite page 108). The neighbors were up in arms because it was seen as more of a threat than an igniter of joy. This Louisville building sends out the wrong environmental message and is a deterrent to revitalization. A much better approach would be to renovate these buildings and turn them over to low- and moderate-income buyers and renters.

Pink Houses

Don't paint it black or white. Paint it pink and create outrage!

What is it about a pink house that can be so polarizing in neighborhoods? Hundreds of years ago, residents in Louisville, KY; Charleston, SC; Havana, Cuba; and Italy used this distinctively feminine and sensuous color to define a house. A pink house is often the highlight of a neighborhood and is a key feature in books on chromatic homes.

Louisville's "Pink Palace," a grandiose clubhouse for men built in 1891 on St. James Court in the Old Louisville neighborhood, was originally red brick. But the building was painted pink by the Women's Christian Temperance Union years later to protest its suspected former use as a place for drinking, gambling, and prostitution. Another makeover in the 1970s brought earth tones to the building's lavish exterior. When new owners decided to return it to bright pink, they were met with a stop order during painting. The owners won their case by proving they were using the traditional paint color of pink. Today, scarlet and neon green highlight the windows and door frames. The "Pink Palace" is one of the highest priced homes in Old Louisville, currently valued at $675,000.

Another famous "Pink Lady" (shown on page 112) is a house on the west side of Louisville where the boxing legend Muhammad Ali, then known as Cassius Clay, grew up. Ali's father, a house painter, outraged neighborhood residents by painting his West Louisville home pink. Like father, like son?

Outrageous, challenging, provocative, and beautiful is the DNA of Muhammad Ali's family. According to family cousin and confidant Dwan Turner, Mr. Clay's pink home sent a message of breaking away from the crowd of white houses. The house continues to convey a message of freedom, beauty, and pride. The decision to paint the house pink was inspired by Martin Luther King, Jr., who led marches through Louisville for freedom, justice, and fairness.

In The Original Highlands, one of the most attractive shotgun houses is done with a pink door and gingerbread embellishments. Another example is The Pink Lady Mansion in Eureka, CA, where the owner painted it pink and prompted protests by residents. Today, it is a signature building in Eureka and a popular bed and breakfast. A bright, cheerful, chromatic home reflects health, vitality, and brightness in a world sometimes dark, unimaginative, and oppressive. Chromatic homes are amazing public art that our major museums have not yet recognized. They are as vital and powerful as what is inside many museums. Rich or poor, just about anyone can turn a broken-down home into a shiny gem.

Paint is cheap, and personal drive, perspiration, imagination, and dedication make up 90% of the effort. This small book was written to inform and inspire, with glimpses from around the world, how color can beautify a home, regenerate a neighborhood, or transform a cityscape. Chromatic homes change the view, from dull to sparkling, from sleepy to vibrant.

Painting a home or a business can spark new life in a neighborhood—even in a city of too much sameness—and offers opportunity to have an oasis of cool. Well-preserved chromatic homes make a city more lovable and beautiful. Think big but start small with your own house! Why not join the joyful color movement and make your own chromatic contribution?

The simple act of painting an old structure in bright or bold colors, thereby turning it into a chromatic home, sometimes empowers the entire block to do the same.

Epilogue: My Lifelong Love Affair with Victorian Homes and the Keys to Neighborhood Revitalization

You can redo the front of your home for as little as $212 and make it more beautiful, valuable, warm, and lovable.

This book highlights the wide range of chromatic homes near and far from Louisville to Moscow. No books have been published citing Louisville, KY; Cincinnati, OH; New Albany, IN; Burano, Italy; or Samara, Russia. Such a book is long overdue.

As Harvey Molotch states, *"Painting houses is a worldwide practice for self-expression. It also cues in that someone of responsibility and concern is around. Color, and its maintenance, can thus be an urban force for confidence."* Similarly, Jeff Speck argues, *"People undervalue the role of paint color in creating community identity, pride, and interest."*

Jane Jacobs argues that nobody wants an undignified neighborhood that is seen as either second- or third-class. Many of today's historic urban neighborhoods face the challenges of urban pollution, crime, brownfields, abandonment, speeding traffic, and treeless streets, but some have tremendous opportunities to become first-class neighborhoods that reflect dignity, pride, joy, and prosperity.

Everyone has an equal right to a livable, safe, sustainable, accessible, and healthy neighborhood. The chromatic home can be the secret sauce for neighborhood rejuvenation. But it needs to be coupled with community organizing that involves sweat, energy, timing, unity, and communication.

Creating an authentic, livable neighborhood can be a key to our happiness.

Chromatic Homes: The Joy of Color in Historic Places

My Story

One of my dreams was to buy an old Victorian and renovate it like the "painted ladies" in my home-town of San Francisco. I loved carpentry and it became a hobby. It seems I took every available wood and metal shop class in high school where I built surfboards (that would not float!), tables, cabinets, book shelves, and an elaborate custom camper for a 1953 Chevy truck.

An apprentice job even came my way with an opportunity to build a complex of homes and recording studios for rock legend Neil Young on his mega ranch along Bear Gulch Road, several miles away from my boyhood home near San Francisco's Crystal Springs Reservoir. The opportunity was a tempting fork in the road for me, but I did not take it because I was only 17 and an even bigger fan of my Dad. My Dad's greatest wish was for me to go to a great University and get a degree, a dream he was never able to fulfill because the Great Depression caused him to lose his scholarship at Columbia University after completing just two years there. My Dad wanted me to have the same excitement and challenge he had experienced in the life of the mind. And I have. Attending the University of California at Santa Barbara, earning all my degrees, and teaching there and other places has been sheer joy.

Looking back at my historic renovation projects, I never thought I was the best at it. It was a hobby and an investment, not a profession. Some of the renovations, gingerbread additions, architectural enhancements, and even the selection of paint colors could have been better. I was compromised by cost considerations and availability of skilled labor, which can be erratic. But for the past 10 years, I have been lucky to have worked with the talented and dedicated Greg Rieck and his team, who have completed most of my renovations.

I think it is important to be candid about my own experience and mistakes, and I have no regrets about investing in and renovating homes. In the end, it's a fragmented partnership with the neighbors, city, banks, preservationists, labor and code enforcement, and even family—everyone has an opinion or a requirement of what needs to be done. The journey certainly made me a better teacher in planning, historic preservation, community development, sustainability, and housing. In many ways, it was the best of all worlds.

I bought my first home in 1989 on First Street in Old Louisville. At the time, First Street was a rough and tough neighborhood with boarded-up houses, and had a high concentration of poor people living in old mansions, sometimes subdivided into ten or more units. First Street was a notorious, multi-lane, one-way street that facilitated prostitution, drugs, and fencing operations.

The purchase price of the Victorian was $36,000; it required new bathrooms, kitchen, paint, and floors, and the third-floor attic was refinished at a cost of $75,000. Ironically, we had a run-in with the historic preservation office, which did not want us to paint over the peeling paint on the brick with bright colors. They wanted us to use acid wash to remove the old paint, which is expensive and often ineffective. The preservation staff's position was overturned by the community board, and the compromise was to have it painted a blue-gray brick tone. It would have looked better if we had been allowed to give it a San Francisco "painted ladies" accent.

Thanks to our improvements, the property sold for $96,000, a loss for the money invested. It was later purchased for $165,000, and the current owners are planning to list it at $299,000. The new price comes four years after the city put in bike lanes, planted trees, and converted some one-way streets to safer two-way streets. A Hispanic grocery store, coffee shop, bakery, child care center, and a pizza parlor later followed, contributing to today's more livable and sustainable neighborhood, and additional small business investments are planned.

Chromatic Homes: The Joy of Color in Historic Places

While the full investment was never recovered, there was enough money from the sale to purchase a bungalow for $85,000 in The Original Highlands in 1990. It had three bedrooms, an enlarged kitchen, a dining room, and a living room. Renovations to this home included converting the attic into a master bedroom and children's bedroom, adding a second bathroom, and setting up a wonderful writing room. The "tree house" (on top of the second floor) reminded me of one of my tree forts from childhood. The property sold for $245,000 after I lived there for 12 years.

These photos show an example of the before-and-after of a home I bought for $150,000 in 2004, turned into a duplex, painted, and marketed for over $300,000. It was featured in The New York Times in 2007 as a Kentucky Derby-week rental, with rents for five days ranging from $2,000 to $8,000, increasing in value with improvements. The upstairs became an Airbnb while I lived downstairs. It was interesting to see that many of the renters were musicians, poets, and several notable authors who wanted a place to write a book, looking for inspiration similar to San Francisco's Alice Walker. But more importantly, this Victorian inspired our neighbors to renovate their steamboat Victorians, and pretty soon the entire neighborhood was taking off.

I purchased another Victorian home for $130,000 that had major code violations, a cracked foundation, and needed a new roof, deck, and plumbing. The city threatened to have it demolished. I completed extensive remodeling, but it never really took off as a rental until the outside was painted with bright colors—pink, red, and turquoise. It was then immediately snatched up by high-end renters. It later sold for $275,000. It seems that chromatic homes *rent* for higher prices, *sell* for higher prices, and are *in high demand* for Airbnb folks.

If people see you earning profit, they might also invest in the neighborhood. The purchase of a house is the single biggest investment many people make, and it may determine what kind of retirement he or she can have. I was eventually able to broaden my real estate holdings, owning 11 homes that were either a single, duplex, triplex, or fourplex.

Pride-of-place is great, but getting a good return makes it worth the effort! Plus, a good return allowed me to do "good things" with it. I invested in a memorial "Butterfly Garden," funded non-profits, and supported playwrights and research assistants. I donated legacy money to the University of Louisville and the University of California. The profits have helped to cover the costs of editing, designing, and printing this book.

But to be clear, it is not shameful or wrong to make a profit from "saving" or renovating an aging home or building, which is a win not only for the owner but for the neighborhood or city as well. I get plenty of teasing about it as a liberal.

A chromatic home can ignite a neighborhood into greater livability, safety, health, and community. It has happened in the once down-and-out Original Highlands, but is it too late for other neighborhoods with many of the same problems?

This book makes the case it is never too late to turn around a house or a neighborhood.

Acknowledgments

We hope to inspire a "paint this neighborhood movement" throughout the world. Why not?

The term "chromatic" was chosen because it has more utility and covers a broader spectrum of buildings than the trademarked "Painted Ladies" (Pomada and Larsen; 1978, 1989, 1992). "Chromatic" allows for different, unique painted styles that go beyond the Victorian designs of San Francisco. My thanks to Michael Larsen, co-author of *"Painted Ladies,"* who loved my book idea and encouraged this distinction. The evolution of this book was in three stages. The first version, *"Our Beautiful Home,"* was designed with the help of Lisa Turner. It covered the history of remodeling and renovating my Victorian home in Louisville. This home (pictured on page 120) ultimately received national and international focus in books, newspapers, and travel magazines, and was featured in The New York Times (Gilderbloom, 2008).

Lacey Gabbard, a graduate student in Urban Planning from the University of Louisville, designed with me the second version of this book called, *"Louisville's Painted Ladies."* It was a 36-page teaser to publishers and immediately received offers for publication from academic and commercial presses. Ultimately, my desire for more control over the book led me to go with local talent. I engaged a highly talented and passionate designer, Leah Callahan—it was great working with her and her Irish instincts to say "no." I also wanted to go local with a printing company, Four Colour Print Group, working with Eric Taylor and Jared Stevens. Thanks to University Press of Kentucky (UPK) for agreeing to distribute our book, and for their helpful tips. Special thanks to Anne Dotson, the Senior Acquisition Editor at UPK, for giving us a long leash to grow the book publishing division of UofL Sustainable Urban Neighborhoods. We thank Steve Wiser for his direction, support, advice, and enthusiasm. Steve has written excellent books on Louisville's historic architecture, modernism, and carriage houses; we hope this book supplements his efforts.

Again, I would like to express gratitude to my friends and colleagues who were gentle critics of my work and who also kept me honest and earnest. I received helpful comments and ideas from Debra Harlan, Matthew Hanka, Jim Ross, Rich Holmer (my stepbrother whose uncle was the late Art Holmer (highlighted in this book), Chad Frederick, Jim Mims, MarJie Ryan, Patty Gilderbloom, Colleen Crum, Richard Jett, Don Jackson, Russ Weaver, David Day, Lyle Sussman, Teresa Jackson (who introduced me to Gaudi and gave me the mesmerizing quote on page 26), City Councilmember David James, Tom Owen (our local historian), Donovan Rypkema, Heather Rypkema, Max Gilderbloom, Andres Duany (a constant inspiration), and my students, neighbors, and fellow New Urbanists. All omissions and errors are those of the author and not the responsibility of any others.

Special thanks to Cary Willis, Kim Crum, Ellen "the original pretty lady from Texas" Slaten, Donna Emerson, and Rick Redding for editing. And finally, a special thank you to Greg Rieck, whose crafts-manship is featured in my Victorian homes. Most of the book's photos (about 85% of them) I took using an old-school Kodak 35mm camera over a 29-year period, along with updated shots taken with a point-and-click digital camera and several shots from my iPhone 6s. Additional pictures were provided by Leslie Sue Gilderbloom Murray, Chuck Woodall, Donna Emerson, David Ames, Jon Lorence (taken during Hurricane Harvey), Stephen Roosa, Ken Chilton, Anthony Campbell, Lesley Patterson-Marx, Justin Smith, Leah Callahan, and Michael Davis. Some photos are not of the highest quality but were the only ones available to make our argument. Apologies to those photos we could not use.

The additional cost of book production was largely funded by donations from Larry Gough and Chase Sorrick of Investment Property Advisors in Louisville; David Day Real Estate; Marilyn Melkonian of Telesis; Jeff Underhill of Underhill Associates; and Louisville City Councilmember David James. Other contributors were purchasers of artwork from the "Cuban Art Exhibit" at Bernie Buren's City Café in Louisville.

This book is dedicated to Donna Emerson who contributed in countless ways and was my inspiration.

"The best people possess a feeling for beauty, the courage to take risks, the discipline to tell the truth, the capacity for sacrifice. Ironically, their virtues make them vulnerable; they are often wounded, sometimes destroyed."

— Ernest Hemingway

References

- California Architects and Builders News, April 1885
- Capitman, Barbara. (1989) Deco Delights: Preserving the Joy and Beauty of Miami South Beach Architecture. New York E.P. Dutton
- Cisneros, Henry G. and Engdahl, Lora (editors). From Despair to Hope: Hope VI and the New Promise of Public Housing in America's Cities. Washington DC: Brookings Institution Press. ISBN 978-0-8157-1425
- Delehanty, Randolph. (2000) San Francisco Victorians. San Francisco: Chronicle Books
- Duany, Andrews. Plater-Zyberk, Elizabeth. Speck, Jeff. (2001) Suburban Nation. New York, NY: North Pointe Press. ISBN 0865476063
- Evanosk, Dennis. Kos, Eric J. (2017) San Francisco: Then and Now. London, UK: Pavilion
- Fitzpatrick, Mary. (2006) New Orleans: Life in an Epic City. New Orleans: published by the Preservation Resources Center of New Orleans
- Florida, Richard. (2002) The Rise of the Creative Class. And How It's Transforming Work, Leisure, and Everyday Life. Basic Books
- Fuster, Jose. (2016) Por qué Jamanitas? Why Jamanitas? Habana, Cuba: Estudi Taller Fuster
- Gilderbloom, John. Mullins, Robert. (2005) Promise and Betrayal: Universities and the Battle for Sustainable Urban Neighborhoods Albany, NY: SUNY Press. ISBN 0791464830
- Gilderbloom, John. (2008) Invisible City: Poverty, Housing, and New Urbanism. Austin, TX. University of Texas Press. ISBN 0292717105
- Gilderbloom, John. (2019) Ten Commandments of Livable Neighborhoods: Creating Healthy, Safe, Prosperous, Just & Sustainable Places Publisher: University of Louisville, Sustainable Urban Neighborhoods
- Goodman, Paul. (1959) Growing Up Absurd: Problems of Youth in the Organized System. New York, Vintage
- Jacobs, Jane. (1961) The Death and Life of Great American Cities by Jane Jacobs. New York: Random House
- Luhan, Gregory. Domer, Dennis. Mohney, David. (2004) Louisville Guide. New York, New York: Princeton Architectural Press
- Malakhov, Sergei. Repina, Evgenia. (2014) Workshops. Samara, Russia: University of Samara School of Architecture (tatlin.ru)
- Michaelson, William H. (1970) Man and His Urban Environment: A Sociological Approach
- Michaelson, William H. (1977) Environment Choice. Human Behavior and Residential Satisfaction. New York: Oxford Press
- Montgomery, Charles. (2013) Happy Cities. Farrar, Straus, Giroux. ISBN 978037416823
- Mouzon, Stephen. (2010) The Original Green: Unlocking the Mystery of True Sustainability. Miami, Florida: Guild Foundation Press
- Pomada, Elizabeth. Larsen, Michael. (photographs by Douglas Keister) (1978) Painted Ladies: San Francisco's Resplendent Victorians. New York: Dutton
- Pomada, Elizabeth. Larsen, Michael. (photographs by Douglas Keister) (1989) Painted Ladies Revisited: San Francisco's Resplendent Victorians Inside and Out. New York: Dutton
- Pomada, Elizabeth. Larsen, Michael. (photographs by Douglas Keister) (1992) Painted Ladies: The Ultimate Celebration of Our Victorians. New York: Viking Studio Books
- Santana, Carlos. (2009) Foreword in Annice Jacoby's Street Art San Francisco: Mission Muralismo. New York: Abrams
- Speck, Jeff. (2012) Walkable City: How Downtown Can Save America, One Step at a Time. New York: Farrar, Straus, and Giroux
- Strutner, Suzy. (2013) Burano, Italy Is the Cheeriest Little Island and It Will Lift Your Soul on Travel Tuesday. Huffington Post, 11/5/2013
- Tyler, Norman. (2000) Historic Preservation. New York, New York: W.W. Norton
- Weinstein, Dave. (2008) It Came From Berkeley: How Berkeley Changed the World. Salt Lake City, Utah: Gibbs Smith
- Westmoreland-Doherty, Lisa. (2008) Louisville Architectural Tours: 19th Century Gems. Atglen, PA: Schiffer Publisher
- Wiser, Stephen. (2016) Carriage Houses of Louisville. Louisville Heritage Publications
- Wiser, Stephen. (2012) Distinctive Houses of Louisville. Louisville Heritage Publications

"House colors don't just boost your mood, enhance the neighborhood, and welcome you. They can increase the value of your home."

— The Color People, Denver, Colorado